2

23
04

PI

Brain Games
LOGIC
PUZZLES

Edward Godwin

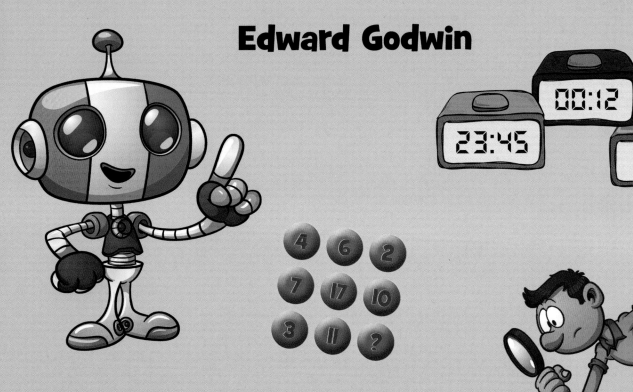
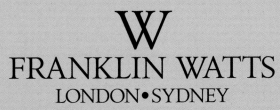

W
FRANKLIN WATTS
LONDON · SYDNEY

First published in 2015 by Franklin Watts

Copyright © Arcturus Holdings Limited

Franklin Watts
338 Euston Road
London NW1 3BH

Franklin Watts Australia
Level 17/207 Kent Street, Sydney NSW 2000

Produced by Arcturus Publishing Limited,
26/27 Bickels Yard, 151-153 Bermondsey Street,
London SE1 3HA

Text: Edward Godwin, Jane Moseley and Jackie Strachan (JMS Books llp)
Illustrations: Memo Angeles and Others/ Shutterstock
Design: cbdesign
Editors: Joe Harris with Frances Evans

Thank you to Miss Rock and Violet Class at Hawkhurst CE Primary School

A CIP catalogue record for this book is available
from the British Library.

Dewey Decimal Classification Number 793.7'3
ISBN 978 1 4451 4152 7

Printed in China

Franklin Watts is a division of Hachette Children's Books, an Hachette
UK company.

SL004334UK

Supplier 03, Date 0115 , Print Run 3864

CONTENTS

DOMINO EFFECT

Which orange domino completes the sequence? Remember to check your answers at the back!

A   B   C   D

RIGHT ON TARGET!

Using the first two targets as an example, find the missing number. (Clue: multiply two numbers...)

A LITTLE BIT BATTY

Which number completes this batty sequence?

1   2   4   8   ?

"X" MARKS THE SPOT

3 ╳ 1
7   5

4 ╳ 2
8   6

7 ╳ 6
3   2

6 ╳ ?
5   1

Find the missing number to complete the puzzle. (Clue: look at the numbers at either end of each line.)

Find the correct number to replace the question mark. (Clue: look at the relationship between the numbers in each segment.)

9 1 7
7   7
9   10
8 4
1 5   14 ?
6 4   8   3
12 9
2   13
13   2
11 16

BOXED AND FOXED

Can you work out which number is missing from the empty crate? (Clue: think in three-digit numbers!)

GREAT SKATES!

Can you work out which number is missing? (Clue: try cutting the circles in half.)

Replace the question mark in this gem with the correct number. (Clue: look at the numbers in the opposite segments.)

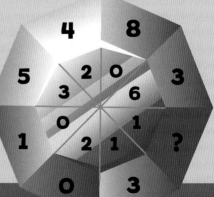

ABSOLUTE GEM!

PAWS FOR THOUGHT

Can you work out which number is missing from each line of animal tracks? Use the top line as an example.

A 3 5 8 12 17 23

B 7 9 ? 16 21 27

C 1 3 6 ? 15 21

D ? 10 13 17 22 28

E 2 ? 7 11 16 22

F 10 12 15 19 ? 30

TIME FLIES...

Which of the digital displays on the right completes this sequence of watches?

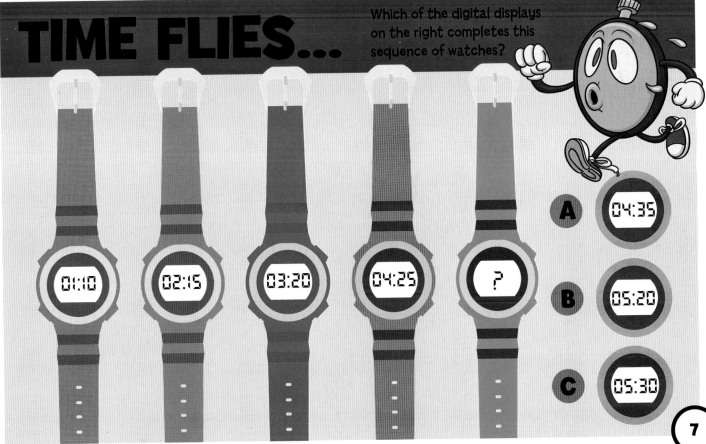

01:10 02:15 03:20 04:25 ?

A 04:35

B 05:20

C 05:30

LET'S GO FLY A KITE!

Which of the yellow kites on the left will replace the one with the question mark? (Clue: don't just look from left to right.)

WHAT'S THE TIME, MR WOLF?

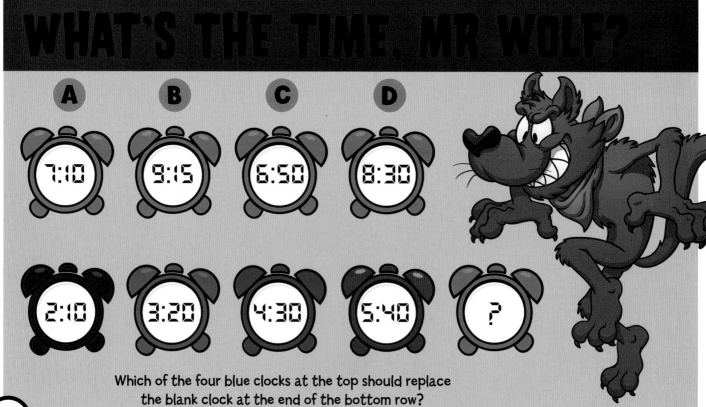

Which of the four blue clocks at the top should replace the blank clock at the end of the bottom row?

ON VACATION!

One label in each suitcase is a misfit. In other words it doesn't follow the same rules or requirements as the others. Can you work out which one it is?

SCARY MONSTERS!

3 6 12 24 ?

Which number will complete this monster sequence?

A stamp dealer bought a rare stamp for 70 pounds, sold it for 80 pounds, bought it back for 90 pounds, and sold it again for 100 pounds.

How much money did he make from all this trading?

STAMP IT OUT!

MOBILE MADNESS

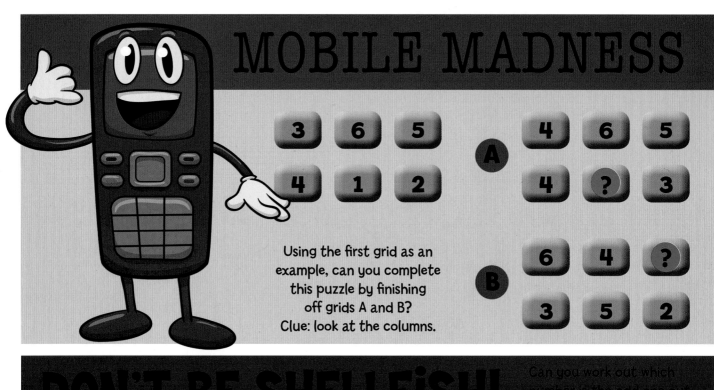

| 3 | 6 | 5 |
| 4 | 1 | 2 |

A

| 4 | 6 | 5 |
| 4 | ? | 3 |

B

| 6 | 4 | ? |
| 3 | 5 | 2 |

Using the first grid as an example, can you complete this puzzle by finishing off grids A and B?
Clue: look at the columns.

DON'T BE SHELLFISH!

Can you work out which number is the odd one out in each group of shells?

15	10	12	20
20	35	55	16	8	28
40	18	10	24

A   **B**

Work out why this puzzle contains these numbers. (Clue: the middle square holds the answer.)

```
        8
    4       10
6       2       15
12    3     5     30
9       4       25
    16      12
        8
```

SPRING HAS SPRUNG...

COUNT LIKE AN EGYPTIAN

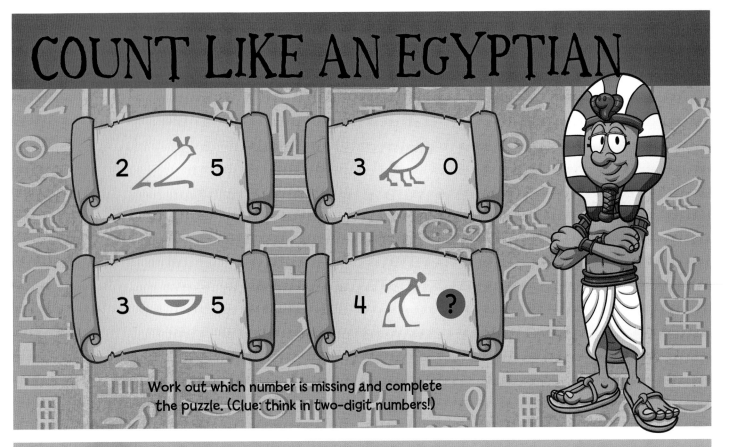

Work out which number is missing and complete the puzzle. (Clue: think in two-digit numbers!)

IT'S SNOW JOKE!

Which of the three snowflakes on the right will complete this puzzle? (Clue: try looking up and down.)

SPOT THE DOTS

Which of the dice on the right (A, B, C or D) should fill the empty space?

A   B

C   D

PIZZA PERFECTION!

Which numbers are missing from the pizza at the bottom right?

(Clue: look at the numbers in the same place on each pizza.)

Which number will complete this sequence?

7   11   13   17   ?

FROM RUSSIA WITH LOVE

JOLLY ROGER

Which number is missing from each skull and crossbones? Check your answers at the back!

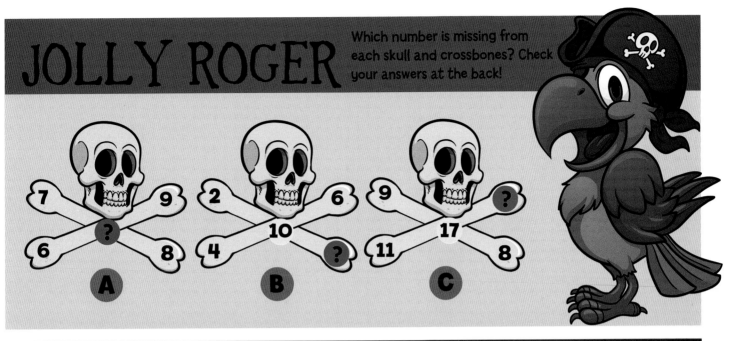

A

B

C

UNDER CONSTRUCTION

Can you find the rogue number in this collection of robots?

5   9   17   24   27

40

5   8

A

63

9   7

B

?

6   12

C

HOLE IN ONE!

Which number goes on the top golf ball of pile C?

13

5 - 4 - 3 - 2 - 1

Look carefully at the sequence of timers and work out the missing number.

GOLDEN OLDIES

Jack and Martha have been married for 50 years and are celebrating their Golden Anniversary. Martha was 19 when she married Jack and Jack is 23 years older than Martha. Can you work out how old Martha and Jack are now?

Can you find the missing number in this wheel? (Clue: look at the numbers in each segment as a group.)

WHEEL OF FORTUNE

PICTURE THIS!

Here is a complete puzzle. Can you work out why these numbers are correct? (Clue, use your addition skills – the middle square is the key.)

TRICK OR TREAT?

Using row A as an example, work out which number is missing from the pumpkins in rows B and C.

Which number completes the web? (Take a look at the pairs of numbers on each segment.)

TIME OUT!

Look carefully at these digital clocks and choose one of the four clocks at the bottom to complete the sequence.

00:01   00:12   01:23   12:34   ?

A 04:56   B 12:56   C 02:34   D 23:45

DINO DILEMMA

In each clutch of dinosaur eggs we have added a rogue number. Can you work out which one it is?

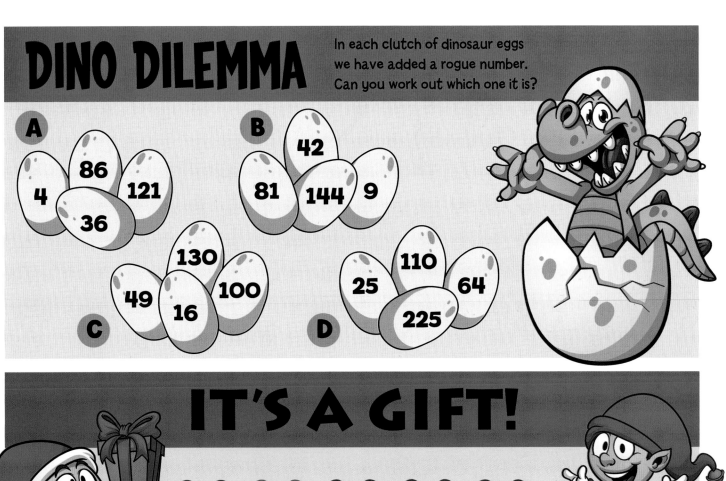

A
4, 86, 36, 121

B
42, 81, 144, 9

C
130, 49, 16, 100

D
110, 25, 225, 64

IT'S A GIFT!

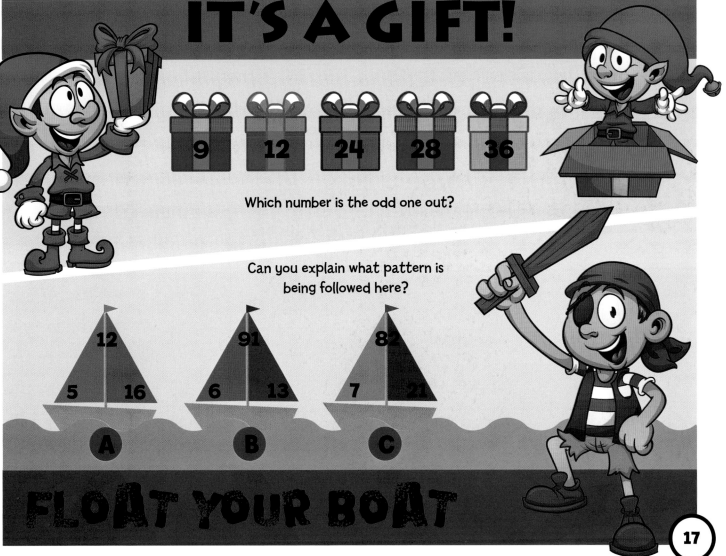

9 12 24 28 36

Which number is the odd one out?

Can you explain what pattern is being followed here?

A — 12, 5, 16

B — 91, 6, 13

C — 82, 7, 21

FLOAT YOUR BOAT

BEACH BALL BONANZA

Which number is missing from the empty segment?

(Clue: look at the matching segments on each circle.)

IT'S MAGIC!

Using the first two stars as an example, find the missing number.

Can you find the missing number?
(Clue: try looking at the numbers in a spiral pattern.)

BIRD ON A WIRE

MONSTER HUNT!

What number is missing from the middle magnifying glass? (Clue: it has got nothing to do with adding or subtracting!)

43　7431　71

29　?　85

68　9862　92

ON CLOUD NINE

Find the missing number. (Clue: think in a spiral!)

1　4　5

60　?　9

37　23　14

19

ABRACADABRA!

Which number is needed to finish the puzzle?
(Clue: think in lines!)

CLOWNING AROUND

By counting the dots on each row of dominoes, can you work out which spare piece completes the pattern?

A   B

C   D

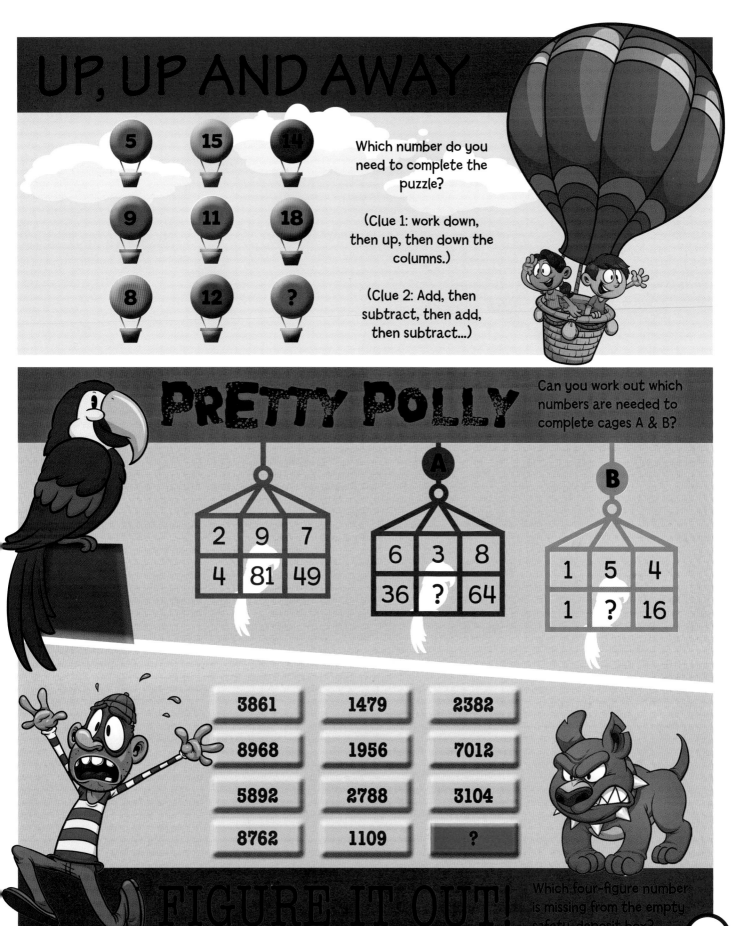

UP, UP AND AWAY

Balloons:
5, 15, 14
9, 11, 18
8, 12, ?

Which number do you need to complete the puzzle?

(Clue 1: work down, then up, then down the columns.)

(Clue 2: Add, then subtract, then add, then subtract...)

PRETTY POLLY

Can you work out which numbers are needed to complete cages A & B?

Cage 1:
| 2 | 9 | 7 |
| 4 | 81 | 49 |

Cage A:
| 6 | 3 | 8 |
| 36 | ? | 64 |

Cage B:
| 1 | 5 | 4 |
| 1 | ? | 16 |

FIGURE IT OUT!

3861	1479	2382
8968	1956	7012
5892	2788	3104
8762	1109	?

Which four-figure number is missing from the empty safety-deposit box?

DICEY DECISION

Three standard dice are shown in the pile on the right. What is the total number of dots on the sides you cannot see? Check your answer when you've finished! (Clue: work out the sum of all the dots on the three dice first.)

PLANET POSER

Can you find the rogue number in each planet?

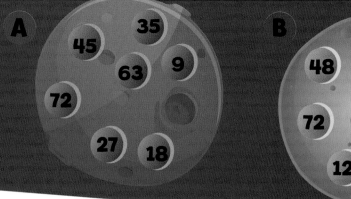

A
35
45
63 9
72
27 18

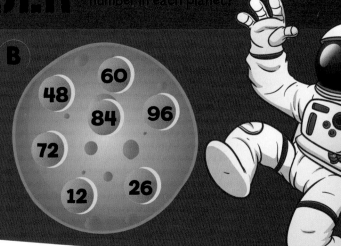

B
60
48
84 96
72
12 26

11:53   02:35   05:23   04:42   12:43

ON YOUR MARKS...

What do the times on these stopwatches have in common? (Clue: look at the digits.)

A-CORNY QUESTION!

2 4 8 16 32 64 128 ?

MAKE A BEE-LINE

1
3   2
7   4
3

4
9   ?
7   8
3

4
3   3

1   2
1

Which number is missing from the empty segment? (Clue: look at the matching segments on each section.)

23

TREASURE ISLAND

A 9 10 12 15 19 24

B 4 5 7 ? 14 19

C 3 4 ? 9 13 18

D 7 8 10 13 ? 22

E ? 13 15 18 22 27

F 122 123 125 ? 132 137

PUZZLED POOCH

Complete this puzzle by finding the missing number. (Clue: try looking at the puzzle from all directions.)

6 10 24

8 12 6

14 22 ?

24

STARS AND STRIPES

Using the first two stars as a guide, can you complete this puzzle?

PARASOL POSER

Find the number that is missing from this parasol. (Clue: look closely at the numbers in each segment.)

Can you find the missing number? (Clue: the puzzle works up and down as well as side to side!)

SPICE OF LIFE

25

SWEET TEMPTATION

4 4
61

7 5
53

6 3
?

Using the first two lollipops as an example, find the missing number. (Clue: when you're writing the answer, think backwards!)

LION'S SHARE

Using A and B as examples, work out what number is missing from pawprint C.

4 12
2 6
A

10 18
6 2
B

7 ?
3 4
C

Each year on his birthday, Toby gets 1 book from his aunt Edwina for every year of his age. That is 1 book on his first birthday, 2 books on his second and so on. Just after his last birthday, Toby counted up how many books he had received since his first birthday, and realised he had 276 in total. How old is Toby?

BOOKWORM

HOW DOES YOUR GARDEN GROW?

Which number is missing from the empty petal? (Clue: look at matching petals.)

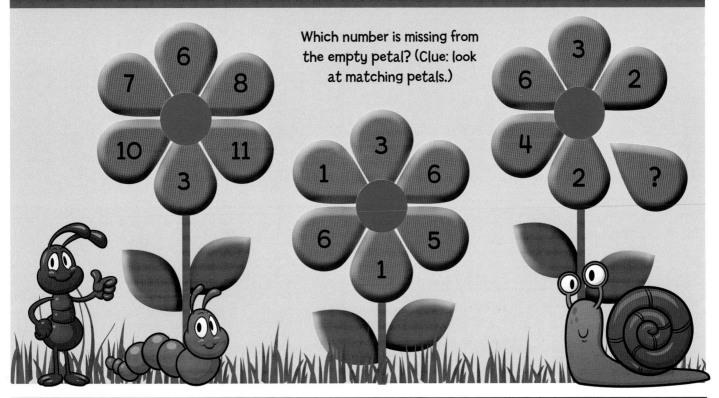

BURGER BLOW OUT!

Which number is missing from the burger in the bottom row? (Clue: try moving in a spiral pattern.)

ANSWERS

page 4

DOMINO EFFECT
Answer = **D**
The dots on the dominoes in the last column equal the total of all the other dots in the same row.

RIGHT ON TARGET!
Answer = **51**
Multiply the top two numbers and write the answer, in reverse, in the bottom segment.

page 5

A LITTLE BIT BATTY
Answer = **16**
Double each number to get the next.

'X' MARKS THE SPOT
Answer = **2**
Add together each pair of opposite numbers to get the same total.

ALL THE FUN OF THE FAIR
Answer = **18**
The number in the middle is midway between the outer two numbers in each segment of the wheel.

page 6

BOXED AND FOXED
Answer = **9**
Read each row as a three-digit number. Starting at the top and working down, the numbers are written in sequence, starting at 100, then 121, 144 and 169. These numbers represent the square numbers of 10, 11, 12 and 13.

GREAT SKATES!
Answer = **16**
One way of doing this is to divide each circle in half, vertically. In each half, multiply the top number by the middle number to give the lower number.

ABSOLUTE GEM!
Answer = **1**
Add up the two numbers in each segment, and add this total to the sum of the numbers in the opposite segment. This always makes 10.

page 7

PAWS FOR THOUGHT
Line B = **12**
Line C = **10**
Line D = **8**
Line E = **4**
Line F = **24**
As you move from left to right, add 2 to the first number, then 3, then 4, etc.

TIME FLIES...
Answer = **C**
The time increases by 1 hour and 5 minutes each step.

page 8

LET'S GO FLY A KITE!
Answer = **12**
In each column, add the top number to the middle number to give the result on the bottom row.

WHAT'S THE TIME MR WOLF?
Answer = **C**
Start with the clock on the left and move to the right. The time on each clock increases by 1 hour and 10 minutes each time.

page 9

ON VACATION
A = **21**
All the other numbers are multiples of 5.
B = **41**
All the other numbers are multiples of 6.
C = **10**
All the other numbers are multiples of 3.
D = **15**
All the other numbers are multiples of 4.

SCARY MONSTERS!
Answer = **48**
As you move from left to right, double the previous number to get the next one along.

STAMP IT OUT!
Answer = **20 pounds profit**
On each deal he made a profit of 10 pounds.

page 10

MOBILE MADNESS
Answer A = **2** and B = **7**
Add the top number to the bottom number of every column to get the same answer for each keypad.

DON'T BE SHELLFISH!
A = **18**
It is the only number not divisible by 5.
B = **10**
It is the only number not divisible by 4.

SPRING HAS SPRUNG...
The outer numbers are all divisible by the inner number.

page 11

COUNT LIKE AN EGYPTIAN
Answer = **0**
Read the two separate digits in each scroll as a whole two-digit number. Moving from left to right, top row then bottom, the two-digit numbers increase by 5 each time, from 25 to 40.

IT'S SNOW JOKE!
Answer = **18**
Moving down the first column, then the second and the third, add 4 each step.

page 12

SPOT THE DOTS
Answer = **D**
In every column and row, the number of dots is counting down from left to right and top to bottom.

PIZZA PERFECTION!
Answer = **7** and **7**
The numbers in each of the segments in the bottom pizzas equal the sum of the corresponding segments in the two pizzas immediately above.

FROM RUSSIA WITH LOVE
Answer = **19**
As you move from left to right, the numbers follow the sequence of prime numbers.

page 13

JOLLY ROGER
Add together the numbers at each end of the bones to get the middle number.
A = **15** 7 + 8 = 15 9 + 6 = 15
B = **8** 2 + 8 = 10 6 + 4 = 10
C = **6** 9 + 8 = 17 6 + 11 = 17

UNDER CONSTRUCTION
Answer = **24**
All the other numbers are odd.

HOLE IN ONE!
Answer = **72**
In each pile, multiply together the bottom two numbers to give the value of the top golf ball.

page 14

5 - 4 - 3 - 2 - 1
Answer = **04:07**
The time decreases by 1 hour and 12 minutes each step.

GOLDEN OLDIES
Jack is 92 and Martha is 69.

WHEEL OF FORTUNE
Answer = **4**
In each segment, add the outer 2 numbers together to give the result at the middle of the segment.

page 15

PICTURE THIS!
Add together the three numbers in each of the outer frames, and then add the number in the middle frame nearest to these three numbers. The total will always be 15.

TRICK OR TREAT?
Line B = **1**
Line C = **6**
In each row, add the first two numbers to get the next number and continue this sequence (2 + 3, 3 + 5, 5 + 8, etc).

page 16

WORLD WIDE WEB
Answer = **8**
Each pair of numbers equals 10.

TIME OUT!
Answer = **D**
The digits move one place to the left each step.

page 17

DINO DILEMMA
A = **86**
B = **42**
C = **130**
D = **110**
All the others are square numbers (2 x 2 = 4, 3 x 3 = 6, 4 x 4 = 16, etc).

IT'S A GIFT!
Answer = **28**
All the other numbers are multiples of three.

FLOAT YOUR BOAT
Add the bottom two numbers together, reverse the digits and the resulting number is placed at the top of the sail.

page 18

BEACH BALL BONANZA
Answer = **4**
The difference between the matching segments in the far left and middle ball appears in the matching segment in the far right ball.

IT'S MAGIC!
Answer = **7**
Add up the outer numbers and divide by 2 get the middle numbers.

BIRD ON A WIRE
Answer = **9**
Starting in the top left corner and moving clockwise in a spiral pattern towards the middle, add 3 for the next number, subtract 1 for the next, add 3, subtract 1, etc.

page 19

MONSTER HUNT!
Answer = **9852**
Take the digits in the outer circles of each line and arrange them in the middle circle, counting down from the largest.

ON CLOUD NINE
Answer = **97**
Start on the top left, and move clockwise in a spiral towards the middle. Add the first two numbers together to give the next one along. Continue around the rest of the pattern of clouds.

page 20

ABRACADABRA!
Answer = **4**
Each line of three numbers, including the middle figure, 1, adds up to 12.

CLOWNING AROUND
Answer = **C**
Moving along the rows, the dots on all four dominoes add up to 18.

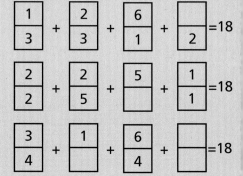

page 21

UP, UP AND AWAY
Answer = **17**
Moving down the first column, up the second and down the third, add 4, and then subtract 1 and repeat those two steps again and again.

PRETTY POLLY
Red cage answer = **9**
Blue cage answer = **25**
Square the top numbers in each cage to get the bottom numbers. (3 x 3 = 9, 5 x 5 = 25)

FIGURE IT OUT!
Answer = **7653**
Each number in the middle column is the difference between the numbers in the first and third columns of the same row.

page 22

DICEY DECISION!
Answer = **38**
There are 21 dots on a dice (1 + 2 + 3 + 4 + 5 + 6 = 21) , so the sum of all the dots on three dice is 63. You can see 25 dots, so the remaining number is 38.

PLANET POSER
Planet A = **35**
It is the only number not divisible by 9.
Planet B = **26**
It is the only number not divisible by 12.

ON YOUR MARKS...
The digits shown on each watch add up to 10 every time.

page 23

A-CORNY QUESTION!
Answer = **256**
Moving from left to right, multiply each number by 2 to get the next number.

MAKE A BEE-LINE
Answer = **6**
Multiply the numbers in the matching segments of the top and bottom honeycomb cells on the right to get the answers in the matching segments in the cell on the left.

page 24

TREASURE ISLAND
Line B = **10**
Line C = **6**
Line D = **17**
Line E = **12**
Line F = **128**
Moving along the rows, add 1, then 2, then 3, then 4 and finally 5.

PUZZLED POOCH
Answer = **30**
Working in columns, add the top number to the middle number to give the bottom number.

page 25

STARS AND STRIPES
Answer = **5**
Starting with the top number and moving clockwise, double each number and subtract 1 to get the next.

PARASOL POSER
Answer = **4**
The numbers in each segment add up to 15.

SPICE OF LIFE
Answer = **12**
Multiply together the first and second numbers in each row to get the third number.

page 26

SWEET TEMPTATION
Answer = **81**
Multiply together the top two numbers and reverse the digits of the answer.

LION'S SHARE
Answer = **14**
On each pawprint, add together the first, second and fourth numbers to find the third number.

BOOK WORM!
Answer = **23 years old**

page 27

HOW DOES YOUR GARDEN GROW?
Answer = **6**
Subtract the numbers in the petals of the middle flower from the numbers in the matching petals of the left-hand flower, giving the results in the right-hand flower.

BURGER BLOW OUT!
Answer = **28**
Starting in the top left corner, move clockwise in a spiral pattern towards the middle. Numbers increase by 3, 4, 5, etc.

GLOSSARY

anniversary A date that is celebrated to remember a special event in a previous year.

bonanza A very large amount.

construction A building or the process of building something.

dilemma A situation where you have to make a difficult decision.

opposite Situated across from something.

parasol A light umbrella used as a sunshade.

relationship The way in which two or more people or things are connected.

rogue Behaving in a way that is not expected.

safety-deposit A box for storing valuable items.

segment A small part of a larger object or shape.

sequence An arrangement of things in a particular order.

subtract To take away one part or number from another.

target A mark (or goal) to aim at.

FURTHER READING

Collins Mental Maths: Ages 9-10 (Collins, 2011)

Geometric Puzzles to Scratch your Brain by C. Mahoney (CreateSpace Independent Publishing Platform, 2013)

Logic Puzzles (Activity Cards) by Sarah Khan (Usborne Publishing, 2012)

WEBSITES

www.bbc.co.uk/cbbc/games/by/type/puzzlegames
Hours of puzzle fun

www.kidsmathgamesonline.com/logic.html
Fun logic games to play

www.thelogiczone.plus.com/logic_index.htm
Logic puzzles to solve

INDEX